– Lil Yah Yah –
I Can Do
Anything

Written and Illustrated by Yahzir Malphurs

Lil Yah Yah has big hopes and dreams.

Lil Yah Yah was always told he can do anything.

One day, Lil Yah Yah had an idea.

He said, "momma, listen to my bright idea."

But his mother said, "Boy I am too busy. Get out of my face."

Lil Yah Yah is a very creative seven-year-old boy. One day Lil Yah Yah said to his mother "can I make dinner tonight; I know how to make burgers?"

His mother looked at him with a grin and asked, "Boy, you got burger money?"

Lil Yah Yah is oh-so-talented, and wanted to show his mother he could read. He said, "Momma, listen to me read this book."

His mother kept cleaning and said,"Yah Yah, you better not lose that school library book!"

Lill Yah Yah, Lil Yah Yah, very athletic Lil Yah Yah.

One day Yah Yah said to his mother, "Momma, come watch me make a jump shot!"

His mother shouted from her bed, "Boy, don't be making that noise!"

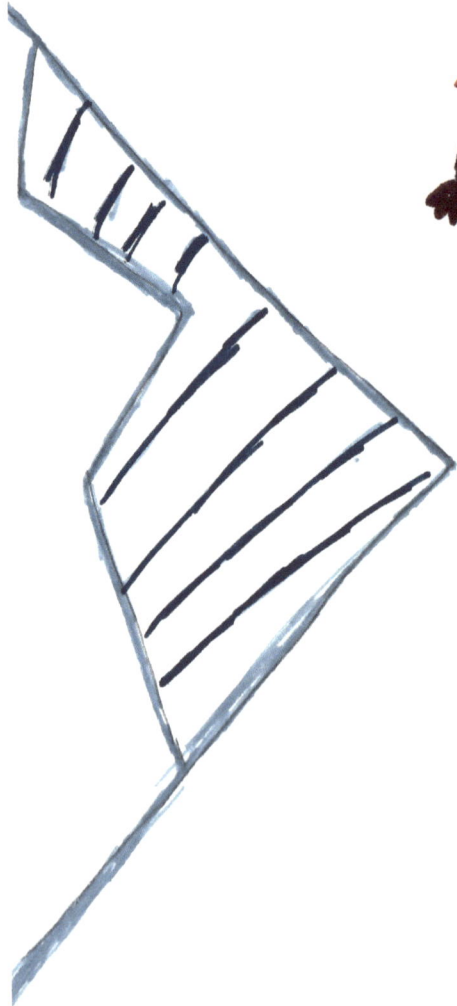

Dance music

Lil Yah Yah what a great dancer he is.

One day Yah Yah said to his mother "Momma I'm a great dancer come and see!"

But instead his mother was too busy doing chores and said, "Boy, sit down before you break your legs."

Lil Yah Yah such a wonderful painter he is.

One day Yah Yah said to his momma, "Let me show you my artwork."

Instead Yah Yah's mother was too busy and said "Boy, you better not get any paint on my floor."

Lil Yah Yah had plans to surprise his Momma for her birthday.

After school he came home, took his bath and rushed to his room. Yah Yah worked all night on his surprise for his Momma.

His Momma yelled, "Yah Yah, you better turn off the lights and go to bed before you are too tired for school tomorrow!"

Lil Yah Yah stayed up all night against his Momma's wishes.

He wrote a short poem and painted a portrait of her.

He drew a nice picture of himself and framed it just for his Momma.

The next morning Lil Yah Yah hid all of the surprises in his book bag and took them to school so he could work on them during lunch time.

Every night after dinner, Yah Yah worked on his painting and his book.

Yah Yah knew this surprise was going to make his Momma proud of him.

Lil Yah Yah's surprise was coming along just swell.

He knew he only had one more day to finish up his projects because his mother's birthday was coming soon.

Yah Yah worked very hard to finish everything up in time.

That night, Lil Yah Yah set his room up in a very special way.

He placed the portrait on the wall.

He placed the book on his desktop so his momma will see it.

He put his picture he framed of himself right where she wouldn't miss it.

Yah Yah knew the surprise would put a smile on his Momma's face.

The day came!

It was finally his Momma's birthday and Yah Yah had to find a way to keep his Momma out of his room, while he went to school so she wouldn't see the surprise he set up for her.

After school he waited for her to arrive home from work.

His Momma always worked late and usually Lil Yah Yah would be asleep by the time she arrived home.

The door opened and Yah Yah was standing with a huge smile on his face.

His Momma said to him, "Boy, what are you still doing up? It's late!"

Lil Yah Yah said, "I have the best surprise for you!"

They both began to walk upstairs but his mother went in her own room to get ready for bed.

Yah Yah began to yell, "Momma! Momma! You have to come to my room quick, I have a huge surprise for you?"

As she walked to his room she said, "Boy what kind of surprise? And stop that yelling!"

Yah Yah flung his door open and yelled "Happy Birthday Momma!"

His mother couldn't believe her eyes and began to cry.

This is so lovely my son but why didn't you tell me you were working on all this?

Lil Yah Yah looked at his mother and said, "I tried to tell you my ideas."

"I tried to let you taste my cooking."

"I tried to have you listen to me read."

"I tried to have you watch me play basketball and dance."

"I tried to show you my paintings."

"I've tried to show you all the things I can do Momma but you were too busy to see them."

Lil Yah Yah turned to his mother and said "I'm glad you love it Momma you always told me I can do anything."

Yah Yah's mother looked at him and said I am so proud of you son, I never knew you were so talented. I will start to spend more time with you then I will know all these great things you are capable of doing.

Lil Yah Yah's mother gave him a big hug.

I am so proud of you and I love you Yah Yah and yes, you can do anything positive if you put your mind to it.

A message from Lil Yah Yah: Please spend quality time with your kids. Let them know they can do anything they put their minds to as long as it's positive.

THE End

www.ingramcontent.com/pod-product-compliance
Lightning Source LLC
Chambersburg PA
CBHW041526070426

42452CB00036B/30